I0845962

The Jesus Code

Computer Programming Lessons from a Divine Source

Table of Contents

Chapter 1. Introduction

Delve into a unique merger of the sacred and the scientific in our groundbreaking Special Report, "The Jesus Code: Computer Programming Lessons from a Divine Source." This comprehensive study is a harmonious blend of theology and technology, offering a refreshing perspective to believers and coders alike. Find out how the tenets of faith can inspire and enrich our understanding of computer programming. Whether you're a seasoned programmer or a spiritual seeker, we promise you an enlightening journey that bridges the gap between the celestial and the coded. Get ready to dive into a realm where advanced technology meets age-old wisdom. Prepare to be inspired and motivated, as this report could prove to be the perfect addition to your library, offering unique insights only a click or two away.

Chapter 2. The Divine Blueprint: Decoding Spiritual Symbolism

It could be said that both scripture and code contain profound layers of meaning, hidden waiting to be decoded by the instructed eye. For both religious and non-religious programmers, understanding the spiritual messages encoded in scripture might provide valuable insights enhancing their coding endeavors.

2.1. Unpacking the Mystery of Spiritual Symbolism

In theology, symbolism plays a pivotal role. It is used as an instructional tool, a way of communicating profound truths and concepts. We find this in parables, visions, and prophetic utterances recorded in sacred texts. Understanding these symbols opens the door to a deeper, more enriched comprehension of the divine narrative.

Symbols, in essence, are types of code. Programmers, as coders of digital realms, will find a familiar landscape here. Just as a symbol encapsulates a profound truth, a line of code can encapsulate a complex process. Recognizing this correlation provides a framework for understanding spirituality and coding as twin studies; both are explorations of hidden truths, wisdom locked beneath the surface.

2.2. The Language of Symbols: A Lesson not in Literacy but in Coding Secrecy

Imagine a passage of scripture as a block of code. Each symbol or event is like a method call, instructing the reader on how to respond or what to understand. For example, in Christianity, the cross is a potent symbol, representing sacrifice, redemption, and salvation. Coded into this symbol are layers of meaning, deep calls to gratitude, humility, and faith.

Programmers understand this concept well. Much like the cross, a single command in a programming language may unleash a sequence of intricate processes beneath the hood. Consider the "print" command in Python. To a non-coder, it simply displays a message. But to a programmer, it signifies a call to the output subsystem, where the operating system manages render objects, memory allocation, and output streams to execute this simple request.

2.3. From Symbol Interpretation to Good Programming Practice

The principle of achieving more with less can be learned from interpreting spiritual symbols. A single symbol can encapsulate a universe of meaning, similar to a single line or block of well-conceptualized code encapsulating complex operations. Aiming for simplicity and conciseness in code cleans the unnecessary clutter, optimizes operation, and makes the code easy to debug and maintain. In this way, the programmer mirrors the theologian's pursuit of understanding through simplicity and clarity.

2.4. The Rituals of the Text: The Beauty of Order in Chaos

In many religious practices, ritualistic reading, re-reading, and meditating on a piece of scripture provides the key to unraveling its coded message. Programmers embark on similar routines when decoding complex bugs or learning new languages.

The methodology of "Scrum" in software development, for instance, promotes regular short meetings (rituals) enabling a collective understanding of what each one is doing and sharing input on tackled challenges. This sense of community and shared wisdom is reminiscent of group scripture studies, where mutual input unearths deeper insights.

2.5. Using Spiritual Symbolism to Enhance Your Programming

Understanding the symbols in scripture can enable programmers to better comprehend the grand design of the universe and apply this wisdom to their coding endeavors.

For instance, the concept of 'synchronization' offers a fascinating parallel: in spirituality, an individual's thoughts and actions must align with divine wisdom, just as in computer programming, processes must synchronize to avoid conflicts. This parallel can inspire programmers to design programs with the same harmony and synchronization evident in the cosmos.

In summary, the interpretation of spiritual symbols provides us with expanded mental constructs for understanding the universe that directly apply to the realm of coding. Whether it is the symbolism of a cross or the functionality of a 'Print' command, the encoded truths unravel themselves to those who have the patience and desire to delve further in their search for understanding.

As we decode the symbolism, we are in a unique position to apply its wisdom to our code, integrating the celestial with the coded to create harmonious, optimized systems reflective of larger, universal principles. This journey into the world of sacred programming has just begun; there's so much more to decode, interpret, and apply.

Chapter 3. Scripture to Script: The Bible as a Programming Manual

Really, programming languages and holy scriptures share a lot more in common than one might initially perceive. Both provide a platform for conveying profound ideas, and they undergo interpretation and execution—be it by a machine or an individual. Viewing biblical texts through the lens of a programming language could offer novel insights and perspectives into each.

3.1. The Similarities: Programming and Religion

Both programming and religion operate on constructs of language, interpretation, and execution. They consist of a language framework, a compiler (interpretation), and an executor (compliance). In religion, the language framework is the scripture. The interpretation is carried out by religious scholars and priests, while the executor is the adherent who acts according to the teachings. In programming, the language framework is the programming language, the compiler is the interpreter, and the executor is the computer operating on that interpreted instruction.

3.2. Code Structure Mirroring Biblical Verses

Each line in a scripture has a context, set of rules, commandments, or teachings to deliver. Similarly, each line of code has a specific function, guided by rules and syntax that allow it to operate within the larger program.

```javascript
// 1 Timothy 5:8
var member = 'anyone';
if (doesNotProvideForRelatives(member) &&
especiallyForImmediateFamily(member)) {
  worseThanUnbeliever(member);
}
```

This script embodies the verse from 1 Timothy 5:8: "But if anyone does not provide for his relatives, and especially for members of his household, he has denied the faith and is worse than an unbeliever." In the script, the 'member' variable is taken through each function, which act as the biblical commandments, and is subject to these rules.

3.3. Scriptural Rules: Setting the Moral Syntax

Rules in programming, like the commandments in the Bible, guide the behavior of entities. Commandments like "Thou shalt not murder" operate in the same vein as rules in a programming language that prohibit certain syntax like "Do not modify constants." Violating these rules leads to undesirable consequences.

3.4. Recursion and Biblical Teachings: Unraveling the Infinite Loop

Just as recursion in computer programming helps solve complex problems by breaking them into smaller, more handleable parts, biblical teachings about love, kindness, and truth, applied repetitively, can help resolve life's more significant challenges.

Consider the concept of forgiveness as instructed in Matthew 18:22. Peter queries Jesus, asking how often he should forgive individuals who sin against him. Jesus responds, "seventy times seven." This is potentially an early illustration of recursion, where forgiveness is not necessarily limited to 490 times, but symbolizes an unbounded, continuously Running loop.

```
function forgiveness(person, numberOfTimes){
  let i;
  for(i=0; i < numberOfTimes; i++){
    forgive(person);
    if(i===numberOfTimes-1){
      forgiveness(person, numberOfTimes);
    }
  }
}
```

3.5. Interpreting Outcomes: From Compile-time Errors to Moral Dilemmas

Just as incorrect or nonsensical code will return compile-time errors, moral actions that do not align with scriptural teachings can lead to undesirable outcomes, much like run-time errors.

Understanding scriptures and coding both involve debugging—an iteration process where the errors are rectified for optimal functionality. Every programming challenge involves assessing what worked and what did not, understanding why, and using this understanding to fix errors for better output. This process reflects the spiritual journey, where individuals strive to better themselves.

3.6. The Efficiency of Algorithms and the Simplicity of Biblical Philosophy

Biblical teachings often advocate for simplicity, be it through the parable of the mustard seed or the love towards one's neighbor. They guide us towards efficient and effective ways to approach life. Similarly, efficient algorithms are crucial in programming as they execute tasks quickly and simplify complex functions.

In conclusion, the relationship between scriptures and programming is profound. While one offers moral, ethical and philosophical guidance, the other provides structured rules to guide problem solving and algorithmic thinking. Both advocate for innovation and evolution: scriptures guide spiritual advancement while programming languages further technological progression. By integrating the two, we can forge a unique path that marries the sacred and the scientific in unprecedented ways.

Chapter 4. Parables and Parameters: Seeking Meaning in the Coding World

In the realm of the religious and the rational, parables occupy a special space. Their iterative nature, the essence they capture, possesses an analogous rhythm to the world of computer programming where incremental approaches are applied to solve complex problems. The lessons one could extract from parables map seamlessly onto the challenges of the coding world, forming a strange and exciting convergence that allows us to view both discourses in a new light.

4.1. Iterative Learning: A Deep Dive

The core practice of breaking down a problem and solving it in increments finds a perfect analogy in the nature of parables. Much like how one interprets and understands a parable, a problem in programming too can be deconstructed and examined from multiple angles before it can be resolved.

A parable unfolds through layers of meanings and interpretations, as does a programming problem through the procedure of iterative debugging. As we peel back these layers in search of a solution, we will encounter obstructions. But the key to both understanding a parable and solving a programming hiccup lies in patience, resilience, and acquiring an intensive understanding of the context.

Therefore, to understand the parables and to comprehend the lay of the programming landscape, an iterative, consistent approach is vital. It invites us to pay attention to the subtle nuances of the essence being conveyed through a parable or the coding problem at hand.

4.2. The Concept of Parameters: Insightful Boundaries

Parameters in coding are not only about specifying factors but also about creating boundaries. Like commandments in religious texts, they set the limits of our actions, guiding our practices. Parameters establish a structure within which programs operate efficiently, reinforcing discipline.

However, parameters, much like commandments, are not absolute constraints. Rather, they guide us by drawing the boundary that incubates creativity, deep thought, and solutions. Parameters invite us to come up with innovative ways to work within the given constraints, thereby triggering the generation of compelling applications and insightful solutions.

4.3. The Truth Lies in Simplicity

Whether it's understanding a parable or solving coding problems, stripping away the complexities to get to the core of the matter is vital. In the world of programming, the simpler and more concise the code, the better it is in terms of understanding, testing, and debugging. Similarly, parables unravel their deepest wisdom when one pares them down to their essential truth.

In both discourses, the significant principle here is that profound outcomes often arise from applying profoundly simple processes. Simple code runs faster and more efficiently, just as simple interpretations of parables could lead to profound wisdom and insights into life's conundrums.

4.4. The Flexibility of Functions and Interpretations

Parables are inherently flexible, open-ended narratives that can be moulded to fit various interpretations. In a similar vein, functions in coding are abstractions that allow for reuse and interpretation in numerous contexts.

This connection between parables and programming points to an often overlooked aspect of both: adaptability. Just as parables adapt and find relevance across cultures, eras, and circumstances, functions in coding allow us to use the same code in different scenarios through parameterization.

Ultimately, in both the realm of spiritual understanding mediated through parables, and the concrete universe of computational tasks managed with programming, the lessons learned go beyond the confines of the immediate context. This mutuality underlines the salience of adaptable principles, open to interpretation and application in differing settings.

As we unfurl the layers of parables and parameters, it becomes increasingly clear that the technologies of the word and of the mind share numerous commonalities. These lessons hold potential not just for improving our understanding of faith and programming, but also helping us tackle problems more effectively. By perceiving these crossovers and interconnections, we can carve a unique conversational path that encourages us to seek meaning and solace within the supposedly disparate worlds of theology and technology.

Chapter 5. Miracles, Algorithms and the Mystical Connection

As we delve deeper into the confluence of spirit and science, it is apt to bring into discussion the pinnacle of divine manifestations - miracles, and juxtapose them with the nuanced world of algorithms. There's a profound correlation waiting to be explored, revealing a mystical connection between the principle of miracles and the ingenious design of algorithms.

5.1. The Nature of Miracles

Traditionally, a miracle is understood as a supernatural event that defies the laws of nature. However, from a theological perspective, miracles are not as much a violation of the natural order as they are a manifestation of the divine order. They are meaningful, purposeful, and intent-driven occurrences designed to show the power and grace of a higher being. They are designed, not to suspend natural laws, but to exceed their limitations, in order to reveal the Love and Mercy that abounds in the Divine Heart and provide comfort and solace to those in need.

In the context of technology, specifically in the realm of computer programming, miracles can be studied by examining the parallels between divine manifestations and the implementation of algorithms.

5.2. The Principle of Algorithms

Algorithms, in the simplest terms, are a set of instructions designed to perform a specific task. While miracles seem to defy logic and natural laws, algorithms exist wholly within the realm of logic. They are a procedural set of steps, intricately designed and arranged in perfect sequences, with an unwavering focus on efficiency and precision. They don't defy laws, but rather build upon them.

The very act of creating an algorithm is akin to a creative miracle. Out of the murky complexities, an algorithm retrieves solutions, quite like a miracle offering resolution in a desperate situation. It is through the application of the algorithm that the incomprehensible becomes comprehensible, and a once unsolvable problem is suddenly solved.

5.3. The Mystical Connection

The connection between miracles and algorithms can be seen when viewed through the perspective of purpose. Just as miracles serve a particular divine intention, algorithms are designed with a specific objective. They are both problem-solving by nature. Just as miracles find solutions to mortal predicaments, algorithms resolve computational complexities.

While miracles are seen as definitive proof of divine involvement, algorithms too bear testimony to the brilliance of the human mind, reflecting its ability to solve problems, innovate, and move beyond perceived limitations.

5.4. A Deeper Examination

A closer look into the mystical connection reveals that both miracles and algorithms operate on the principle of causality - a cause-effect relationship. For miracles, the cause is divine will and the effect is the occurrence of the miraculous event. For algorithms, the cause is the initial conditions or input, and the effect is the computed outcome. Both represent a transition from one state to another, uniquely manipulated to offer a meaningful outcome.

Algorithms, like miracles, are intent-driven. They are designed to not only resolve a problem but to do so in the most efficient and effective way; to reach the most optimal state of resolution, just as miracles work to create the most spiritually meaningful outcomes.

5.5. Embracing the Synthesis

This analysis helps us comprehend that sacred phenomena and scientific principles are not competing or contradictory ideas. Instead, they can converge and complement each other, broaden our understanding of the universe, and enrich our problem-solving abilities.

Understanding the correlation between the divine principle of miracles and the logical principle of algorithms can enhance our programming skills, making it more nuanced, empathetic, and purposeful. After all, in essence, programming is a quest for solutions, and what better guide than the one that has been solving the unsolvable since the dawn of time.

5.6. Conclusion

Thus, the communion of the sacred and the scientific, particularly the mystical connection between miracles and algorithms, is further proof that the realms of theology and technology are not mutually exclusive. Instead, they can exist in a symbiotic relationship, with each shining a light on the other, enriching the human understanding and paving the way to a more enlightened future.

Chapter 6. The Sermon on the Mount: A Lesson in Problem Solving

The full chapter content for "The Sermon on the Mount: A Lesson in Problem Solving" begins as follows:

New Testament Scripture abounds with lessons on life's commonplace challenges, yet these biblical narratives hold deeper, transformative wisdom that we can apply to areas seemingly unrelated to faith. The Sermon on the Mount is one such profound teaching. Christ's discourse, known for its ensign call to 'turn the other cheek', is a masterclass in creative problem solving. Let us delve into it with a programmer's lens.

6.1. The Beatitudes: Foundational Values for Problem Solving

The Sermon commences with the Beatitudes, which induce a shift in thought from the standard paradigms of success and wellbeing. Blessed are the poor in spirit, those who mourn, the meek, those who hunger and thirst for righteousness, the merciful, the pure in heart, the peacemakers, those who are persecuted for righteousness' sake.

In the realm of programming, we can reflect on the Beatitudes in unique ways. The poor in spirit may be those who maintain humility about their coding prowess, constantly developing their skills, and adapting to new paradigms. Similarly, those who mourn could be empathetic developers who recognize, lament, and strive to remedy the problems technology can cause in society.

The meek in programming are the ones willing to work behind the

"

scenes, coding for the sheer passion of it and not for recognition. Those who hunger and thirst for righteousness may reflect ethical hackers and activists using their coding skills for the greater good. The merciful are tolerant programmers, understanding that everyone, including themselves, makes mistakes and takes time to grow.

The Beatitudes then could serve as a compiler of moral code, checking our attitudes and enhancing our approach to problem solving.

6.2. Retaliation and Love for Enemies: A Different Perspective on Dealing with Bugs

In the section on retaliation and love for enemies, Jesus teaches a counterintuitive approach - to turn the other cheek. He says, "If anyone strikes you on the right cheek, turn the other also." And extends the philosophy to love your enemies. This cryptic message holds the secret to a more effective approach towards problem solving.

Often, when faced with bugs or errors in code, our initial reaction is to attack back defensively. We may hastily patch the bug or blame the software, hardware, or even colleagues. We may view the error as an enemy. What if we instead respond with patience, curiosity, and love?

Taking time to understand the bug, instead of hastily fixing it, can lead to root-cause analysis and a more reliable solution. Treating bugs as learning opportunities, imagining them as teachers rather than enemies, can foster a more fruitful, less stressful coding environment.

6.3. Ask, Search, Knock: The Power of Commissioning Help

One effective method of problem solving cited in the Sermon is to ask, search, and knock. In programming, many encounter problems their current set of skills cannot solve. At these times, developers can take a cue from the Sermon's wisdom, not hesitating to ask for assistance, search for solutions in documentation or forums, and knock on the virtual doors of community spaces. They may approach project leads or colleagues, recognizing that important solutions often emerge from collaboration and dialogue.

6.4. Building a Stable Codebase: The Wise and Foolish Builders

The concluding parable, of the wise and foolish builders, emphasizes the importance of a robust foundation. In programming, this speaks to the need for a well-structured, clean codebase. Building software upon a hasty, unstable codebase is like the foolish man building his house on sand, leading to disastrous results when storms or unexpected bugs hit.

The wise programmer, however, mirrors the man who built his house on rock. They invest time upfront to design a solid architecture, write clean and maintainable code, perform thorough testing and code review, and continually refactor their code. Such a codebase remains robust and reliable through changes in requirements, new feature additions, or software evolution.

In conclusion, Christ's Sermon on the Mount, universally lauded for its spiritual and moral instructions, seamlessly intersects with key principles of problem-solving in the realm of coding. It encourages programmers to uphold values of humility, empathy, passion, ethics, tolerance, and patience, to take a constructive approach towards errors, leverage the power of community assistance, and build upon a solid foundation of a clean, robust codebase. Applying these principles can lead to software creation that is not just functionally effective but also socially aligned and personally fulfilling.

Chapter 7. Compiler of Compassion: The Beatitudes in Binary

The Beatitudes, as treated in the Gospel of Matthew, provide a spiritual framework for goodness, kindness, and compassion. When viewed through a computational lens, such as in the coding realm, these teachings can be enlightening, influencing conscious coding and compassionate compiler design. In this chapter, we aim to decipher these Beatitudes from binary to an understanding that promotes effective and empathetic programming methods.

7.1. Compassionate Coding - A Basic Premise

Before there were computers, there was human language, which enabled us to communicate complex and profound truths about our existence. Jesus's teachings have long stood as timeless principles for leading a compassionate life. Considering these principles from a coding perspective can help us develop software that embodies the same qualities of grace, mercy, and kindness.

7.2. The Beatitudes in Binary

Consider the Beatitudes as an array of guiding principles for life, or, in coding terms, a set of functions. In the binary system, the most fundamental language of computers, everything comes down to a series of 0s and 1s, on and off, true and false. Translating the essence of the Beatitudes into binary constitutes a unique approach to understand basic moral values in relation to computer processes.

Blessed are the poor in spirit - In binary terms, this could be seen as those who have zero ego, where '0' symbolizes their humility.

Blessed are those who mourn - In binary, this could be interpreted as those who know how to turn off their personal desires ('0') to comfort others in their time of need.

7.3. Christ-like Compiler

A compiler's primary function is to translate the source code, written in a high-level language, into machine code. Going by Beatitudes, a compassionate compiler should function with fairness, diligence, and empathy, effectively translating human intentions into machine-understandable instructions.

7.4. Unselfish Compiling

"Blessed are the meek: for they shall inherit the earth."

Instructions in a program ought to be meek, working in concordance with each other, striving not for superiority but for accomplishing a shared goal as effectively and efficiently as possible. Code should be unselfish, prioritising collective performance over individual lines of instruction.

7.5. Empathetic Debugging

"Blessed are those who mourn: for they shall be comforted."

Just as mourning in the Beatitudes represents empathy towards suffering, empathetic debugging involves understanding and caring about the problem at hand. Segmentation faults or syntax errors aren't just mindless errors; instead, the software is communicating it needs attention.

7.6. Merciful Optimalization

"Blessed are the merciful: for they shall obtain mercy."

Optimalization should show mercy on system resources. Efficient code not only runs faster but also minimally utilizes resources, showing mercy on power usage and overall system demands.

7.7. Pure in Logic

"Blessed are the pure in heart: for they shall see God."

Pure functions in functional programming return the same output for the same input without any side effects, signifying a kind of purity. Similarly, 'purity in heart' calls for transparency, predictability, and integrity in our programming logic.

7.8. Peacemakers in Coding Paradigms

"Blessed are the peacemakers: for they shall be called the sons of God."

Different programming paradigms - functional, logical, procedural, object-oriented - have different strengths. The 'peacemakers' in programming would be those techniques or elements that harmonize these different paradigms, minimizing their shortcomings while maximizing their strengths.

These are merely initial explorations on how to fuse the timeless wisdom of the Beatitudes with coding principles. There is an unending scope for finding deep connections between spirituality and technology, and the exploration of this relationship has the potential to positively influence the coding practices and the software we create.

Chapter 8.
Transubstantiating Code: The Intersection of Faith and Function

Understanding the parallel between faith and coding might initially seem farfetched. Yet upon closer examination, the commonalities start to unravel. Transubstantiation in theology refers to the transformation of one substance into another, its purest sense visible in Christian eucharistic liturgy where bread and wine become the body and blood of Christ. When applied to programming, transubstantiation can be recognized as converting data from one form to another. This chapter seeks to analyze and interpret these similarities and more significantly, how they can inspire us to become better programmers.

8.1. Faith, Transubstantiation, and Its Relevance to Coding

Transubstantiation, a term primarily associated with Christianity, has profound implications when viewed from a coder's perspective. The principles behind this miraculous transformation celebrate the virtue of faith — one's belief in the unseen, the abstract. Believing in something beyond the physicality and our perception is the cornerstone of faith, and it coincidentally, is what every programmer exercises each time they sit behind a computer.

When programmers write code, they are essentially transubstantiating abstract thoughts into concrete functions. The syntax and algorithms are the external symbols, much like the bread and wine. But the core logic or the functionality is like the body and blood of Christ—the essence that provides meaning to these symbols.

8.2. Coding: The Physicality and The Metaphysical

As coders, we constantly shuffle between the physicality of code (the syntax, the structure) and the metaphysical aspect (the logic, the purpose). A simple symbol or character can control a complex action, similar to individual bread and wine elements embodying the divine.

Reiterating this process allows us to subtly reshape our outlook towards programming. It shifts our perspective from seeing coding as mere typing commands to a computer to a more intrinsic act of transubstantiating our thoughts into actuality. It enriches the process and reinforces the profound connection between the physical act of coding and its metaphysical implications.

8.3. Lessons from a Divine Source: Embracing the Unseen

The concept of transubstantiation teaches believers to accept the unseen, which can be an invaluable lesson for programmers. A great deal of programming is about dealing with abstraction and unseen processes that take place within the heart of digital systems.

To embrace the unseen is to not fear the complexities of abstraction, but to understand that it forms the cornerstone of coding. It's about the mastery of utilizing known elements to harness the power of unseen operations, just like transubstantiation uses known entities (bread and wine) to make perceptible an unseen reality (body and blood of Christ).

8.4. The Unfathomable Chaos: Lessons in Debugging

In faith, the concept of chaos is considered to be an aspect of the divine, an unknown puzzle to be worked through. Similarly, debugging in programming is also about dealing with disorder, deciphering it, learning from it, and finally restoring order.

Debugging, therefore, becomes more than troubleshooting. Looking at it through the lens of faith, it resembles an iterative, transformative process that contributes to refining our thinking and improving the software.

8.5. Encapsulated Divinity: Learning from Object-Oriented Programming

Finally, let's turn to Object-Oriented Programming (OOP), a methodology that promotes encapsulation— much similar to how the divine is believed to be embodied in the worldly symbols of bread and wine. OOP teaches us to enclose data and functions within objects, not unlike how the essence of the divine is enclosed in the elements of the Eucharist.

Understanding the intersection of faith and function thus encourages us to see coding as more than a technological process. It gives us a broader perspective, offering spirituality-infused insights and concepts influencing our approach towards programming. We venture beyond the conventional and embark upon a process of transformation—transubstantiation—of our thoughts, ideas, and wisdom into a tangible, coded reality that everyone can experience.

Chapter 9. Reflections on Redemption and Recursion

Recursion, a tool prevalent in both computer science and mathematics, is the process of defining a problem or the solution to a problem in terms of a simpler version of the same problem. On the spiritual side of things, redemption comprises the central theme of forgiveness in Christianity, expressed through the life, death, and resurrection of Jesus Christ. In both processes, we encounter the essence of a 'loop' - in recursion, it's a loop in the logic, in redemption, it is the cycle of sin and forgiveness.

9.1. The Recursive Cycle

The recursive concept in computer programming refers to a function or an algorithmic process that calls upon itself to solve a problem. Recursion is all about working your way down to a more straightforward sub-problem, solving it, and then building up towards the original problem's solution. To understand recursion, one needs to understand that it is fundamentally about perspective.

To illustrate, consider this classic problem: How do we calculate factorial of n (n!)? The factorial of a number (denoted as n!), is the product of all positive integers less than or equal to that number. Mathematically, it is solved as $n! = n * (n-1) * (n-2) * \ldots * 3 * 2 * 1$.

Using recursion, the same problem can be solved by defining it in terms of a simpler version of the problem: $n! = n * (n-1)!$.

One might ask, doesn't this definition seem circular? But that is the brilliance of recursion. It expresses a complex problem using simpler or smaller instances of the same problem.

9.2. The Cycle of Redemption

In an analogous sense, the Christian doctrine of redemption mirrors recursion's cyclic nature. Redemption, in Christian theology, is fundamentally rooted in love and forgiveness exhibited through the life cycle of Christ: his birth, suffering, death, and resurrection. This cycle goes on perpetually, offering the believers constant opportunities for redemption - to sin, seek forgiveness, and be redeemed.

Every Christian, guided by the teachings of Christ, strives towards a moral and ethical life but does falter at times, thus entering a state of sin. However, Christianity doesn't leave the fallen in despair. It offers them a way out - it offers them a chance for redemption, a return to the state of grace.

Repentance and forgiveness form the crux of this redemption cycle. When a believer sins, he repents for his actions, asks for forgiveness to God, resolves not to commit the sin again, and thus, is redeemed. He turns away from sin (recursive base case) and embarks on a journey toward God (the recursive step).

9.3. Recursion in Redemption

The believer's journey to redemption starts with the acknowledgment of sin, followed by repentance, restitution where possible, and then culminates in forgiveness. This is the spiritual recursive case. If we were to chart a similar process for a recursive function, it would look much the same – beginning with the awareness of a problem (equivalent to the acknowledgment of sin), breaking down the problem to simpler sub-problems (repentance), solving the sub-problem (restitution), and then building the solution to the entire problem (forgiveness).

In both recursion and redemption, the process can repeat almost indefinitely until a base case or condition (in programming, a problem that can be solved without further recursion; in spirituality, the absence of sin) is reached. In either context, there's a level of trust involved – trust in the process. For recursion, trust that each recursive call is taking us closer to the solution. For redemption, faith that sincere repentance brings us closer to God.

9.4. The Overarching Connection

Despite their apparent differences, recursion and redemption share a profound connection, a shared essence of cyclical journeys. Both processes embody the concept of reiteration towards a desired state: in recursion, it's a solution, while in redemption, it's salvation. They testify to the fact that to solve complex challenges, whether in programming or in life, the journey often requires us to tackle and overcome simpler versions of the same challenge.

Indeed, these iterative and transformative journeys, marked by failures, lessons, and triumphs, reflect the intricate and interconnected relationship between the scientific and the sacred. And in these moments of convergence, we find the meeting point of spirituality and technology.

In conclusion, reflections on redemption and recursion offer exceptional insights into how the sacred and scientific can complement and provide a better understanding of each other. As we tackle more complex problems in computer programming or, more broadly, life, the ideas of continually focusing on simpler versions, reflecting, and trying again are pivotal. They are the underlying tenets of both redemption and recursion, serving as subtle reminders that the path to any solution, sacred or scientific, often involves stepping back, breaking down, understanding, and relentlessly pursuing till we solve for the base case.

Chapter 10. From the Cross to the Cloud: Salvation through Seamless Code

For eons, human plight has raged on, capturing the hearts and minds of many. In an attempt to find meaning in the melee, theories abound. Some presume the solution to be a connection to a celestial power. Others submit technology holds the key to salvation, preferring the exploratory depth of code rather than the spiritual depth of prayer. Arguably, one might find a harmonious coexistence where faith meets code. This fusion may be seen as a realization of divine order within the regulations of programming language.

10.1. A Brief History of The Cross and The Cloud

The notion of salvation, embodied in the symbolism of the Cross, directly contrasts the visual of the Cloud. One symbol resonates with images of sacrifices, mercy, and divine intervention, while the other with cloud computing, securing data, and code repositories. Seemingly incompatible, these realms, when paired together, offer a unitary vision united by seamless code.

How do we get there? Let's first traverse through time to comprehend the birth pangs of this unlikely marriage.

In scriptural accounts, the Cross was a pivotal point, a turning tide in the age-long conflict between good and evil. To Christian believers, the Cross was where a divine solution to a chaotic problem was presented. Fast forward a few millennia, and we encounter the Cloud - the pivotal point in the technology revolution. A symbol of change, innovation, and progress in the digital age. Thus, a thread begins to weave, connecting the spiritual with the technological.

10.2. Unraveling The Meeting Point

Salvation was delivered on the Cross as a final product, completed and ready for acceptance. Cloud-based technology, similarly, has dynamically transformed how data is accessed, stored, and shared — an innovation made readily available to all. In both instances, the medium changed the established order, creating previously inconceivable opportunities. The Cross made connection with the divine accessible; The Cloud made information universally available.

In this parallel, we begin to explore the syntactical correlation between spiritual doctrines and coding paradigms.

10.3. The Cross: A Lesson in Abstraction

The Cross's unifying power derives from its abstract nature. It conveys the idea of salvation abstractly, negating the necessity of understanding the full complexity of divine plans. For believers, faith forms the foundation of their interactions with the divine, much like abstraction in programming.

InThe pragmatic programmer, abstraction is key to tackling complex problems. Scenes from the gospels where Jesus utilized parables — a form of abstraction — to convey complex spiritual truths, mirrors this concept. By reducing complex topics to a simple narrative, comprehension became achievable, just as complex systems in coding are handled through abstraction.

10.4. The Cloud: Replication and Redundancy as Pathways to Salvation

Redundancy is usually discouraged in programming circles; however, the Cloud invites us to reconsider. The Cloud as a computing architecture prioritizes replication and redundancy to ensure data safety and integrity. How can this replicate salvation?

When code is running in the Cloud, an error in one server doesn't stop the program. Another replica picks it up and continues, providing fault tolerance — a representation of how mistakes don't end our salvation journey. A classic example of the redundancy principle is seen in the biblical verse where Jesus declared seventy times seven forgiveness - a superfluous act of mercy that echoes Cloud redundancy.

10.5. Inspirations from Divine Forgiveness: Error Handling

The concept of forgiveness underlies the notion of salvation. Jesus, while on the Cross, asked his Father to forgive those who crucified him. In programming, error handling would be our equivalent of forgiveness.

Good programmers build a system that fosters an environment of forgiveness. The software should be forgiving enough to handle user and system errors gracefully, using practices like exceptions and defensive programming. This approach ensures that one fault doesn't derail the entire system, teaching us that in life too, individual mistakes don't have to ruin the whole.

10.6. Prospecting Further Associations

Probing the realms of faith and technology reveals a world where divine wisdom can inform and inspire the rigors of code. The Cross and the Cloud, far from being incompatible, offer us a model of thinking that boosts our quest for practical and spiritual solutions. This pursuit presents a roadmap outlining how the sacred can inspire the scientific — and vice versa. It's a field awaiting exploration, teeming with opportunities for future scholars, theologians, and programmers.

As we've begun to uncover, salvation in code doesn't reside in isolation from our spiritual quest. Instead, it completes the quest, ensuring the evolution of thinking that straddles two worlds with perfect ease. This exploration into the correlations may be a pioneering effort to reconcile the sacred and the scientific in an inclusive conversation about our collective future.

Chapter 11. Resurrection and Debugging: A Journey Towards Perfection

Resurrecting and debugging: these seemingly incongruous concepts find common ground in a unique landscape, where theology and technology not only coexist but enrich each other in powerful, compelling ways. Let's explore this symbiotic relationship and supercharge our journey towards perfection.

11.1. The Concept of Resurrection in Theology

The existential fabric of nearly all religions is defined by the concept of life after death, whether it is reincarnation, resurrection, or spiritual awakening. The Christian concept of resurrection, in particular, is central to our discussion. Within Christian theology, resurrection refers to Christ's miraculous rising from the dead, signifying redemption and renewal, and offers the possibility of eternal life.

Resurrection suggests a beautiful, hopeful sentiment: no death is final, no mistake is irreversible, and it is possible to rise again, purer and more refined. It symbolizes a new beginning, a fresh start from a point of apparent end — much like debugging in the realm of code.

11.2. Understanding Debugging in Programming

Debugging in programming parlance is akin to finding and fixing bugs — errors, flaws, or faults — that prevent a computer program from functioning effectively. It is the process of resurrecting code; restoring its health and vitality, and thereby, giving it a new lease of life. As such, debugging signifies a journey towards perfection, a pathway to transforming a sickly, error-riddled program into a healthy and efficient machine.

11.3. Parallels between Resurrection and Debugging: Life, Imperfection, and Hope

When a coding project is riddled with bugs, it's as if the code is "dead" — it cannot function as intended, it cannot deliver its promises. Debugging becomes its resurrection, finding and eliminating bugs and faults that prevent the code from properly functioning.

Much like resurrection, debugging starts from an admission of imperfection — a recognition that there's a fault, a bug lurking in the depths of your code that needs to be addressed. This is simultaneously a humbling and a hopeful stance. It is humbling because it demands acknowledgment of one's limitations, an admission that we are capable of making mistakes. Yet it is also hopeful because inherent in this acknowledgment is the belief that change and improvement are possible.

11.4. The Debugging Process: A Step-by-Step Guide

Now, let's explore the process of debugging in more detail:

1. Recognition: The first step, as with resurrection, is recognizing that a problem exists. One might encounter an error message, an unexpected output, or no output at all. The symptoms of a

problem can vary widely, and learning to recognize these signs comes from experience and understanding.

2. Locating the error: Having identified that an issue exists, the next step is to determine its cause. This involves critically analyzing the output and tracing it back to the line of code causing the problem, often using tools like debuggers and log files.

3. Understanding the issue: Once the problematic line of code is found, it's important to understand why it's causing an issue. This can involve delving into the specifics of programming languages, exploring how different components of the system interact, and researching potential causes of the error.

4. Generating a fix: Having understood the problem, one can devise a solution. This could involve fixing a typo, altering an algorithm, or even redesigning a segment of the system.

5. Testing: The final step is to test the fixed code to ensure the problem is solved and that no new ones have been created. This repeats the cycle, returning to recognition and ensuring the resurrection of the faulty code into functional code.

11.5. Redemption in Debugging: Lessons for Programmers

The process of debugging doesn't only produce a more perfect code; it's also a learning experience for the coder. Each bug offers an opportunity to learn about new pitfalls, better programming practices, or deeper nuances of the system. In debugging, coders learn to be humble in the face of their missteps, tenacious in the pursuit of perfection, and patient as they navigate the labyrinth of code.

Much like embodied believers who strive for spiritual elevation following the path illuminated by the sacred scriptures, programmers too seek redemption and perfection through the journey of debugging. Across theology and technology, resurrection and debugging embody a profound life lesson: whatever the challenge, with patience, knowledge, and grace, renewal and perfection await.

11.6. Embracing Imperfection: The Fuel for Perfection

Just as resurrection embraces the reality of death while symbolizing renewal, debugging acknowledges the inevitability of coding errors and offers a pathway towards perfection. Each bug is just another opportunity for resurrection — a moment of failure that precedes success.

Embrace each flaw within your code. View each misstep as an essential stepping stone towards a flawless code, a perfect system. Much like spiritual enlightenment, the journey towards coding perfection is attained not without trials and tribulations, but through them.

11.7. Conclusion: Resurrection, Debugging, and the Pursuit of Perfection

So, there it is. The journey towards perfection is not solitary; it's a beautiful dance between resurrection and debugging, between an exploration of our weaknesses and the celebration of our potential.

In the coding universe, each bug is but a momentary pause, an opportunity for resurrection. Every flaw encountered and rectified is a step towards perfection. Each time your code 'dies', it merely awaits a resurrection — a debugging — to spring back to life, stronger, wiser, and better.

The sacred and the scientific come together in this remarkable synthesis of resurrection and debugging. Just as Jesus rose from the dead to redeem humanity, so can our 'dead' code rise, renewed and perfected, through the process of debugging. And in this cycle of death and rebirth, we inch closer towards perfection, in code as it is in life.

www.ingramcontent.com/pod-product-compliance
Lightning Source LLC
Chambersburg PA
CBHW060853260726

48661CB00008B/3245

9798856170237